G000255251

Sho

Epping Forest

Guide to 20 enjoyable walks

This book is specially produced for the City of London Corporation
by Collins, an imprint of HarperCollins Publishers
Westerhill Road
Bishopbriggs
Glasgow G64 2QT

www.harpercollins.co.uk
First edition 2018

Printed in China by RR Donnelly APS Co Ltd

ISBN 978 0 85 203092 9
10 9 8 7 6 5 4 3 2 1

email: roadcheck@harpercollins.co.uk

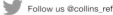 Follow us @collins_ref

Acknowledgements
Photographers: Julian Birch; Clare Eastwood; Keith French; Bob Good; Richard
Manning; Tayla McLuskie; Brian Pallett; Mark Powter; Chris Shepherd; Layton
Thompson; David Woodfall; Alan Woodgate; Yvette Woodhouse

MIX
Paper from
responsible sources
FSC™ C007454

This book is produced from independently certified FSC™ paper
to ensure responsible forest management.

For more information visit: www.harpercollins.co.uk/green

Contents

▶ Short walks

66 Come and enjoy the amazing variety within Epping Forest, London's largest green space. Twenty easy walks reveal the diversity of this ancient landscape and its surprisingly rich history 99

Bluebells, Chingford

Introduction

This ancient Forest, stretching some 19 km (12 miles) from Manor Park in east London to Epping in Essex, is London's largest open space. A former Royal Hunting Forest, today the Forest is some 2,400 hectares (6,000 acres) of historic landscape, and is protected by the 1878 Epping Forest Act. Epping Forest is owned and managed by the City of London Corporation as a Registered Charity.

The Forest is of national and international conservation importance and home to over 50,000 ancient trees and 100 lakes and ponds. The traditional uses of the Forest have created a diverse mosaic of habitats that include historic wood pasture, green lanes, ancient pollarded trees, heathlands and grassy plains, many of which have been grazed for centuries.

Epping Forest is open 365 days a year and is free to visit, with the exception of a charge for horseriders.

Chingford Plain

Walking in Epping Forest

There are almost 100km (60 miles) of surfaced and unsurfaced trails. There are also accessible paths at High Beach, Jubilee Pond, Knighton Wood and Connaught Water. In addition, there are a number of waymarked walking routes. A small number of public footpaths and bridleways also cross the Forest.

Getting to Epping Forest

Chingford, Highams Park, Leytonstone High Road, Manor Park, Walthamstow, Wanstead Park, Wood Street and Woodgrange Park

Buckhurst Hill, Epping, Leytonstone, Loughton, Roding Valley, Snaresbrook, South Woodford, Theydon Bois, Wanstead and Woodford

M25 Junction 26 or M11 Junctions 4 or 5 and head for the A104.

E4 7QH - The View

There are a number of car parks around the Forest. Please visit our website for a full list www.cityoflondon.gov.uk/eppingforest

Wildlife in Epping Forest

Epping Forest is internationally important for the large number of very old trees, mainly oak, beech and hornbeam, and the rare insects, plants, bats and fungi associated with them. Two-thirds of Epping Forest is designated as a Site of Special Scientific Interest.

Great crested grebe

The Forest's ancient pollarded trees have resulted from the tradition of lopping branches for firewood from above head height so that the new growth sprouting from the trunk is out of the reach of grazing animals. Pollarding can prolong the life of a tree. Many are hundreds of years old and support a wealth of rare insects and fungi.

A number of the Forest's trees are known as 'coppards'. This refers to trees that were once coppiced, cut to ground level, but were then allowed to grow to such a height as to allow pollarding.

Common lizard

The Conservators have a legal duty to manage the Forest in such a way as to preserve and enhance the features important for its conservation, including its biodiversity and habitats.

If you encounter an injured animal, call 020 8532 1010 (24hrs).

Buffer Land
In addition to the Forest, the City of London owns some 736 hectares (1818 acres) of Buffer Land adjoining Epping Forest to add further protection to the Forest and maintain links to the wider countryside.

Much of the Buffer Land is accessible on foot by using the public rights of way, permissive rights of way and permissive open access for walking areas.

Before you set out:
- Always try to let others know where you intend going, especially if you are walking alone;

- Be clothed adequately for the weather and always wear suitable footwear;

- Always allow plenty of daylight time for the walk, especially if it is longer or harder than you have done before;

- Be aware that much of the Forest is shared use – expect to meet horses, cyclists and other users;

- Don't leave valuables in your car;

- Carry some water with you.

Summer meadow

The Countryside Code

The Countryside Code is a reminder of how to behave in the countryside and applies to the Forest too. For further information, visit www.gov.uk

Epping Forest Byelaws

In addition to the Countryside Code, Epping Forest is covered by its own Epping Forest Byelaws. See website for further information.

Map reading

The Official Map of Epping Forest is used in this guide. The map is available to purchase from any of the Forest Visitor Centres.

Forest Visitor Centres

Please visit the website for opening times: www. cityoflondon.gov.uk/eppingforest

The View
6 Rangers Road,
Chingford, E4 7QH
Tel 020 7332 1911

The View, with its informative displays and regularly changing exhibitions, is the perfect place to start your exploration of Epping Forest.

Queen Elizabeth's Hunting Lodge
Rangers Road, Chingford,
E4 7QH
Tel 020 7332 1911

The Hunting Lodge is a Grade II* listed building built for Henry VIII in 1543, and is an amazing survival of an intact, Tudor hunt standing.

The Temple
Wanstead Park, E11 2LT
Tel 020 7332 1911

The Temple, a Grade II listed building, dates from the 1760s.

The Temple, Wanstead Park

It was a garden feature in the grounds of palatial Wanstead House and now houses displays on the history of Wanstead Park..

Epping Forest Visitor Centre
Paul's Nursery Road, High Beach, IG10 4AE
Epping Forest Visitor Centre at High Beach houses informative and interesting displays spanning the history of the Forest.

Barn Hoppitt

History

Epping Forest is an ancient Forest extending northwards from densely populated Manor Park and Forest Gate in east London to agricultural Essex. As a former Royal hunting forest, it has played host to Kings and Queens of England.

In the 19th century, the City of London Corporation fought to save the Forest from destruction. Epping Forest has been owned and managed by the City of London Corporation since 1878 when the Epping Forest Act protected it in perpetuity for the recreation and enjoyment of its visitors.

As well as a mosaic of habitats from woodpasture, and deep ancient woodlands packed with veteran oaks and beeches, to acid grasslands and heath, the Forest has a rich human history. There are seven listed buildings, two registered historic parks and gardens and three Scheduled Ancient Monuments within the Forest.

Things to do

Football
Forty-four football pitches including mini soccer, junior and adult pitches, are available to hire.

Cycling
Epping Forest is open to cycling, please ring your bell or call to any pedestrians/horse riders on approach. Please take note of unauthorised areas where exclusion notices are displayed.

Fishing
Epping Forest has over 100 man-made lakes and ponds, with fishing permitted on 24 of them. Fishing is not permitted from 15 March to 15 June. Please do not fish in prohibited ponds. Anglers must have a current Environment Agency Rod Licence.

Golf
The City of London provides an 18-hole public golf course at Chingford. The course is broadly laid out in two returning loops, and plays a maximum 6342 yard, par 72. The course is generally described as challenging with pleasant walking. www.chingfordgolfcourse.co.uk

Horse riding
Epping Forest is a great place in which to ride. A valid horse riding licence must be displayed. Licences can be obtained from The View. Seasonal and other restrictions may apply.

Chingford Golf Course

Autumn hack

Events
A range of events and exhibitions take place at the Visitor Centres and in the Forest. Please visit our website for further information.

Further information
For further information, please visit our website
www.cityoflondon.gov.uk/eppingforest

The Warren
Loughton
Essex
IG10 4RW
020 8532 1010

 @CoLEppingForest

 Epping Forest City of London

 coleppingforest

Epping Forest is a Registered Charity, No. 232990

Butler's Retreat

How to use this book

This book contains route maps and descriptions for 20 walks, with areas of interest indicated by symbols (see below). For each walk particular points of interest are denoted by a number both in the text and on the map (where the number appears in a circle). In the text the route instructions are prefixed by a capital letter. We recommend that you read the whole description, including the fact box at the start of each walk, before setting out.

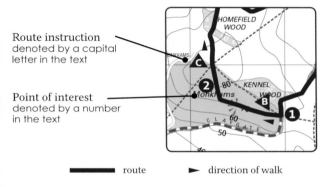

Route instruction
denoted by a capital letter in the text

Point of interest
denoted by a number in the text

▬▬▬ route   ► direction of walk

Key to walk symbols

At the start of each walk there is a series of symbols that indicate particular areas of interest associated with the route.

🐦 Birdlife   ☀ Good views   🐾 Other wildlife

🚣 Boating   🏰 Historical interest   🌼 Wild flowers

🦌 Deer   📖 Literature   🌳 Woodland

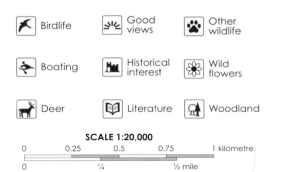

SCALE 1:20,000

0	0.25	0.5	0.75	1 kilometre

| 0 | ¼ | ½ mile |

Please note the scale for walk maps is 1:20,000 unless otherwise stated
North is always at the top of the page

> **"A fascinating walk opening a window to the effects of WWII on this part of Epping Forest"**

The wide open space of Wanstead Flats has been a place of recreation for east Londoners ever since it was drained, levelled and grassed by the City of London Corporation after 1878. During the Second World War (WWII) it was given over to a variety of civilian and military uses. These included allotments, anti-aircraft gun batteries, barrage balloons and bomb shelters. One area became a troop assembly point during the invasion of France in 1944 and another a prisoner of war camp. This walk uncovers evidence of the important role Wanstead Flats played in the conflict.

Barrage balloon tethers at Wanstead Flats

Wanstead Flats in wartime

Route instructions

A Leaving Wanstead Park Rail Station, turn right and head north along Woodford Road to reach the start of Epping Forest. Take the path ahead past the pond.

1 Bandstand or Angel Pond, named after Lewis Angell who constructed it in 1894, was a fashionable spot in Edwardian times. In WWII the pond was filled with debris. The tree circle beyond it marks the site of the bandstand, used as a collection point for wood salvaged from damaged houses and to sell surplus food grown on the allotments, which stretched to the east. A public trench shelter was nearby.

Wanstead Flats in summer

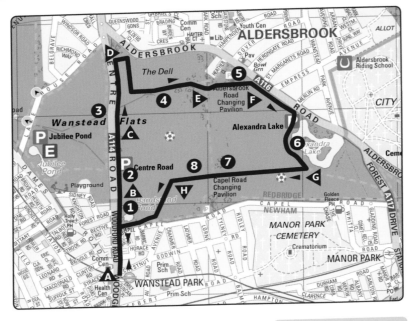

B Continue ahead to the car park.

2 The ditches may be remnants of defence works. Wanstead Flats were criss-crossed with 3ft ditches and turf was rolled up to hinder the landing of enemy aircraft. This area was used by the military as a vehicle park for its heavy vehicles.

C Take the track, later a footpath, with Centre Road to your left, until you reach a gate.

3 The section of the Flats across the road was the site of a prisoner of war camp,

surrounded by a barbed wire fence. The prisoners of war were detailed to do construction work or clear bomb damage. The last of the goalposts erected by prisoners of war remained near to Centre Road until 1998.

D Turn right to follow the track leading around The Dell (a former brickfield) past a copse of trees.

4 Hidden in the trees are the footings of Nissen Huts, about 50 metres apart. The eastern one is said to have housed telephone equipment and operators.

Wanstead Flats in wartime

▶ Walk ahead to a junction of the paths and then skirt the side of the playing fields to reach the rear of the Changing Rooms.

5 This was the site of a large transit camp for both British and American troops preparing for the D-Day invasion. They were marched to ships at the West India Docks for forward passage to Normandy.

F Walk between the football pitches across to Alexandra Lake. Here bear right, over the sandhills surrounding it.

6 The sandhills were used to fill sand bags for putting out fires from incendiary bombs. Sand had apparently been brought here from the Essex coast to make an artificial beach for local families. The slopes also provided a training ground for despatch riders.

G After the second sandhill there is a view of the Gothic gateway to the City of London Cemetery, over to the left. At point G on the map, turn right to walk straight across the Flats alongside more football pitches.

7 The first copse of trees (right) is by the site of an anti-aircraft gun battery, whose multi-firing guns made an almighty noise. Later in WWII, rocket launchers were hidden in bushes during the day and used at night. The site was hit twice during 1944. Beyond the trees and to the right, four metal posts form a rectangle which may have been used to tether barrage balloons. Barrage balloons were dotted around the Flats. Their main purpose was to hold up wires to prevent precision bombing by low-flying enemy aircraft.

H Follow the path leading left, through the circle of trees and continue ahead to return to the station.

8 In summer months you may hear skylarks singing overhead.

Wanstead Flats

66 Explore the southern reaches of Epping Forest –
a burst of green in London's East End **99**

A walk of two parts – through a dense woodland that
formed part of the 18th-century estate of the once famed
and grand Wanstead House, and then across the western
fringes of Wanstead Flats, a wide open space long popular
with east Londoners for recreation, to enjoy views of wildlife
around a rejuvenated pond.

Bush Wood and Jubilee Pond

Small red damselfly

Route instructions

A From Leytonstone High Road Rail Station, cross over Leytonstone High Road and walk down Ferndale Road to reach Wanstead Flats. Continue ahead but shortly turn left down a broad grassy avenue fringed first by bushes and then by trees.

1 Broad avenues of trees once radiated out from the magnificent Wanstead House. This one survives in its original form but many of the trees (limes and sweet chestnuts) have had to be replaced over time.

B At a post bearing an arrow, overlooked by a large white block of flats, turn left and continue in the same direction to emerge on Bush Road, by the Quaker Meeting House.

2 The block, built in the 1960s to house police cadets, replaced a Victorian Swiss chalet, built on the banks of the Great Lake on the Wanstead House estate. In the middle of the lake was Lake House, which lent its name to the Edwardian housing development built over it. The poet Tom Hood lived in Lake House in the 1830s.

3 Quaker Meeting House – on this site was a 19th century archery ground, with lodge, where Charles Dickens gave some of his famous readings. This became a Quaker Meeting House in 1871 and was rebuilt in 1968. The burial ground behind includes the headstone of the prison reformer Elizabeth Fry, moved here from Barking.

Plan your walk

DISTANCE:
3 miles (4.5 km)

TIME:
1.5 hours

START/END:
Leytonstone High Road Rail Station

PARKING:
Surrounding streets

TERRAIN:
Easy – woodland and grassland tracks

NEAREST STATION:
Leytonstone High Road Rail Station

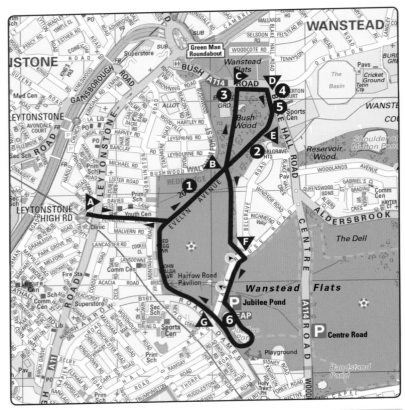

C Walk by the side of Bush Road to the traffic lights at the junction of Blake Hall Road ahead.

4 The road opposite is flanked by two stone gateposts which once gave access to Wanstead House.

D Take the track leading past the old Keeper's Lodge, bearing left near a pond.

5 A few metres short of the Lodge on the left is the footing of an old water fountain. This was erected over a spring used in Jacobean times, when Wanstead was briefly a spa.

E At Evelyn Avenue turn right. On reaching a tarmac footpath, turn left along it then right onto a track which leads behind the gardens of houses on the Lake House estate.

Bush Wood and Jubilee Pond

F Cross over Lake House Road with care and turn right towards the traffic lights. At the car park take the surfaced path that leads to Jubilee Pond. Here turn left to walk clockwise around it.

6 Long used for sailing model yachts, Jubilee Pond was so named in 2002 to mark the Golden Jubilee of Queen Elizabeth II. Extensive work was undertaken to reshape it into its current form as a wildlife habitat thronged with birds.

G Cross back over Lake House Road at the lights and follow a path alongside Harrow Road, turning past the changing rooms up the edge of the Flats to reach Ferndale Road for the return to the station.

Foxglove

66 Magical Wanstead Park, beautiful at any time of year but especially so when the bluebells emerge **99**

Tranquil, sylvan Wanstead Park once formed part of the grand gardens surrounding Wanstead House, a magnificent Palladian mansion torn down in the 1820s. The estate's rich and varied history includes royal connections in Tudor and Stuart times and the tragic story of the last heiress Catherine Tylney-Long who married a Regency rake. Over two centuries the Repton designed garden features have reverted to a more natural forest state but some remain to be found on this walk.

Bluebells, Wanstead Park

Wanstead Park

Route instructions

A From Wanstead Underground Station, turn left along The Green and walk down St Mary's Avenue, turning left into Overton Drive past classical St Mary's Church and the former stables of Wanstead House (now the golf club). Turn right into Warren Road, which ends at the Park entrance. Take the wide track to the left from the car park.

B Take a track to your right, lined with logs, into Chalet Wood.

1 In April this area is carpeted with bluebells, which flourish in the dappled sunlight beneath the tree canopy.

C Emerge onto a grassy plain by The Temple. Turn right and walk down the double avenue of sweet chestnuts, a 1990s replanting of an 18th-century feature.

2 The Temple was built in the early 1760s and housed the estate's groundsmen.

Plan your walk

DISTANCE:
5 miles (8 km)

TIME:
Approximately 2.5 hours

START/END:
Wanstead Underground Station

PARKING:
Surrounding streets

TERRAIN:
Easy - surfaced tracks and natural woodland

NEAREST STATION:
Wanstead Underground Station

The Temple

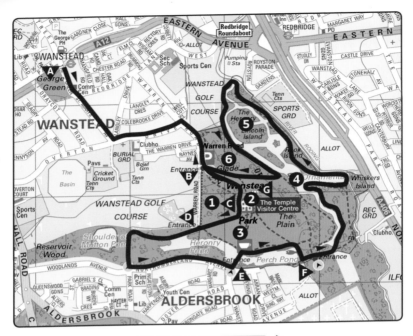

After the City of London Corporation purchased the Park in 1880, two families of Forest Keepers lived here until 1960. It was extensively repaired in the 1990s and now operates as a Visitor Centre, open at weekends, telling the story of Wanstead House and Park.

D Continue ahead with Heronry Pond to your left. The track veers left at the end of the lake and comes out into Northumberland Avenue. Walk left, along the road, re-entering the Park at the next entrance.

E Walk ahead to the Tea Hut with a wide view over Heronry Pond and its birdlife. Turn right here along the edge of Perch Pond to the dam.

3 The open ground to your left is sprinkled with anthills, a rare example in Epping Forest of acid grassland. Look out for green woodpeckers that feed and 'bathe' on the ants, which is a behaviour thought to rid the birds of external parasites.

F Once you cross the dam go left along a wide track that leads to the foot of the Ornamental Water. Here

Wanstead Park

turn left keeping the Water to your left. Follow the path all the way around the long lake, looping back round on the opposite side.

4 A view of The Grotto can be enjoyed across the lake. This romantic folly, built at the same time as The Temple, once served as a boathouse with a cave-like room above, decorated with mirrors, glass and shells. It was destroyed by fire in 1884.

5 Look out for herons on Lincoln Island. The birds migrated here from Heronry Pond. Servants dressed in naval uniform staged mock sea battles on the lake here, watched by guests seated on a grass amphitheatre behind it, now overgrown.

G Turn right on a track through a wide expanse of grass fringed either side by woodland. This leads back to the Warren Road entrance to the Park.

6 This formed the main axis of the gardens. The straight 'canal' behind us dates back to the period of the formal garden design and there are two viewing mounds in the woods on either side. Wanstead House itself was sited at the top of the rise, where today you will find the golf course.

Heron

The Grotto

> **❝** This gentle walk takes you around charming Hollow Pond and across the open expanse of Leyton Flats, one of the most popular areas of Epping Forest **❞**

This easy walk is suitable for families with children as well as anyone wanting to explore this popular landmark set amongst ancient oaks, holly, yellow gorse and grassland. It loops up and over gentle gravel hummocks and around Hollow Pond giving the chance to observe waterfowl. During the summer you can hire a rowing boat.

Egyptian goose at Hollow Pond

Hollow Pond

Route instructions

A At Leytonstone Underground Station, take the High Road Leytonstone exit, noting the Alfred Hitchcock murals in the subway and cross the road. Follow the road towards the High Street and turn left at St John's Church. Continue along the High Road to the Green Man Interchange and the underpass which leads to the Forest. Turn left at the centre of the Interchange, follow the route up onto Whipps Cross Road.

1 Leytonstone High Road marks the route of an ancient track. The stone in the name refers to a mileage marker, an 18th century obelisk which is believed to have replaced a Roman mile stone.

Reflections in Hollow Pond

Great crested grebe

walk
4

Plan your walk

DISTANCE:
4 miles (6.2 km)

TIME:
1.25 hours

START/END:
Leytonstone Underground Station

PARKING:
The Boat House car park

TERRAIN:
Easy

NEAREST STATION:
Leytonstone Underground Station

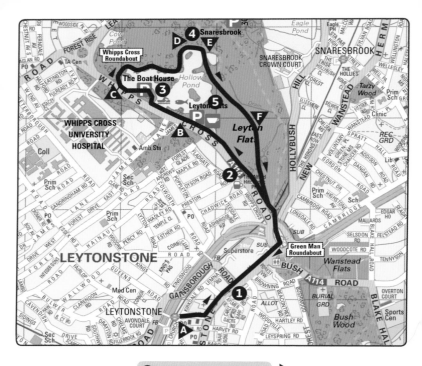

2 Observe the Sir Alfred Hitchcock Hotel looking over Leyton Flats. Alfred Hitchcock, the famous Hollywood director, was born at 517 High Road Leytonstone on 13 August 1899.

B Continue along the hard surface shared pedestrian and cycle path (alongside Whipps Cross Road), a Quietway created to provide access to the Olympic Games in 2012, until you reach a car park. Head into the car park and take the path leading through the trees alongside Hollow Pond.

C Take a clockwise circuit of Hollow Pond passing the boathouse, where boats can be hired. The meandering track closest to the shoreline gives the best view of the water and its wildlife.

3 Hollow Pond was formed in 1883 from water filled pits left by 19th-century gravel extraction. It was enlarged twice over the next 20 years to create a beauty spot and the boating lake featured in many Edwardian photographic postcards.

Hollow Pond

▶ At the eastern end of the water walk round a large bay with a small island offshore.

4 Just to the left is the site of a swimming pool created from another area of old gravel pits in 1905. By 1932 it had been renovated by local councils to become Whipps Cross Lido, very popular with locals. It closed in 1982 and was filled in and reverted to Forest. Swimming is no longer allowed in the Forest ponds.

▶ At the end of the bay you will notice another smaller pond. Keep this to your left and continue around the shore line, passing three abstract wooden play structures.

5 Enjoy watching a range of waterfowl both in and out of the water. You are likely to see Canada geese, coots, cormorants, Egyptian geese, grey herons, mallards, moorhens and tufted ducks.

▶ Take the diagonal path across Leyton Flats towards the Green Man Interchange where you first entered the Forest, and so return to Leytonstone Underground Station.

Geese and rowers

Summer flowers

> ❝ This walk highlights the ancient woodland and history of Epping Forest to be found snuggled cheek by jowl alongside the urbanisation of east London ❞

This varied walk starts in the Snaresbrook Road car park near Eagle Pond and crosses some pleasant sections of the Forest.

Gilberts Slade and Walthamstow Forest

Route instructions

A With nearby Eagle Pond on your right, leave the car park and cross Snaresbrook Road and follow the ride towards Waterworks Corner.

1 Eagle Pond, previously known as Snares Pond, was formed in the early 18th century by damming the valley of Snares Brook. Looking south, behind the pond, is Snaresbrook Crown Court, originally built in 1843 as an infant orphanage. It was designed by Sir George Gilbert Scott and William Bonython Moffatt.

2 It is not known who Gilberts Slade was named after but the word 'Slade' is an old name for an open glade.

B Pass under the roundabout and follow the track heading west to Waterworks Wood and the bridge crossing the North Circular Road.

C Cross the bridge over the North Circular Road and head north towards Mill Plain, where the ride forks, turn left.

Plan your walk

DISTANCE:
4 miles (6.2 km)

TIME:
1.5 hours

START/END:
Snaresbrook Road car park

PARKING:
Snaresbrook Road car park

TERRAIN:
Mixture of surfaced tracks and woodland trails

NEAREST STATION:
Snaresbrook Underground Station

Hornbeam leaves

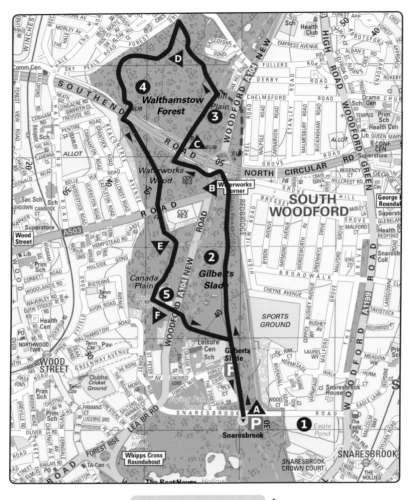

3 Mill Plain is close to the site of Walthamstow windmill which was here from 1676 to 1800, when it blew down. Nearby is a memorial stone to the evangelist, Gipsy Smith, who was born in a tent and raised in a Gipsy camp near this stone.

D Follow the ride in a circular route and once again cross under the North Circular Road and continue along the ride and over a footbridge.

Gilberts Slade and Walthamstow Forest

4 Walthamstow Forest was once extensively used by commoners of the district to provide grazing for their cattle.

▶ Follow the ride across the open area of Canada Plain and take the path veering left after Bulrush Pond towards Woodford New Road.

5 Bulrush Pond was once a boating lake and Canada Plain a well-used picnic area as it was near the terminus of the horse-trams that used to bring visitors to the Forest in the 1880s.

▶ Cross the road to Gilberts Slade, turn right at the T-junction, back to the start of the walk.

Gipsy Smith's stone

> **This tranquil 'island' of Epping Forest has a distinctive charm all of its own**

Knighton Wood and Lord's Bushes, divided by the ancient thoroughfare of Monkhams Lane, have very different histories. Lord's Bushes contains an unusually large population of veteran trees, including oak, hornbeam and beech and has for centuries been in the Forest. Knighton Wood was formerly enclosed and became the woodland garden of Knighton House before it was returned to the Forest in 1930. Evidence of the garden remains.

Knighton Wood Lake

Knighton Wood/ Lord's Bushes

Route instructions

A Start at Buckhurst Hill Underground Station and turn left along Victoria Road, crossing over the junction of Queens Road into Princes Road. At the Three Colts pub, turn left into Kings Place and enter Lord's Bushes by the playground.

B From the playground, turn left down the hill. Cross a bridge and continue straight ahead, bearing right but ignoring the small paths leading off to the right.

1 Much of this area is a relic of the formal gardens of the Buxton Estate. There are still many recognisable landscaped features to spot on your visit.

DISTANCE:
1.75 miles (2.8 km)

TIME:
1 hour

START/END:
Buckhurst Hill Underground Station or Knighton Wood car park*

PARKING:
Buckhurst Hill Underground Station and Knighton Wood car parks*

TERRAIN:
Easy with gentle slopes over woodland areas and some uneven ground

NEAREST STATIONS:
Buckhurst Hill and Roding Valley Underground Stations

Pulpit Oak

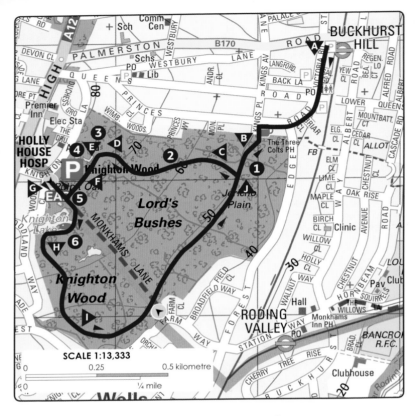

C Continue to a more open area where you will see a waymark post, and follow the arrow pointing right. You are now on the waymarked Rowan Trail. Follow subsequent posts and take the direction indicated by the arrows.

2 The historic Jericho Plain has been extended as part of wood pasture restoration. Old oaks are evident.

D Follow the next waymark post pointing left, at the western edge of Lord's Bushes, along a wide track.

3 There are still some 300 veteran trees to see on your way round, including pollarded oaks and hornbeams, as well as ash, crab apple, elm, field maple, hawthorn, rowan, sycamore and yew.

Knighton Wood/ Lord's Bushes

E Leave the track when you see another waymark post pointing left on a path along the edge of a pond.

4 This pond, a circular crater, was created by a bomb or parachute mine during the Second World War.

F Follow the path until you emerge on Monkhams Lane, where you will see another waymark post. If you follow the arrow to the right, you will reach Knighton Wood car park*.

5 Monkhams Lane is an ancient trackway following the old Anglo-Saxon boundary between the historic Manors of Woodford and Chigwell. Toward the car park is the Pulpit Oak, with a girth in excess of 5m, making it one of the largest-girthed trees in the Forest.

G To continue your walk, retrace your steps back down Monkhams Lane joining the Easy Access Path on the right, evident by the wooden edging to the path. Follow the arrow continuing round the southern side of the lake.

6 You will see Corsican pine and bamboo, evidence of the woodland garden of the now demolished Knighton House. Pulham Stones may be seen at the edge of the lake. These 'stones' (which are in fact composed of a masonry core with a cement-like render) were very popular in the period when the Victorians attempted to mimic nature. The lake was created by Edward North Buxton, a Verderer of Epping Forest, who owned Knighton House.

H At the end of the lake, follow the next waymark post pointing left and continuing straight down the hill.

I Towards the bottom of the hill, follow the waymarked post, crossing Monkhams Lane and continue to follow the arrows until you arrive at Jericho Plain.

J Go straight on, ignoring the next waymark post, which was seen earlier. Cross the footbridge and go straight up the hill to the playground and retrace your steps to the start of the walk.

Hornbeam pollard

*If you start at Knighton Wood car park, follow one of the Forest's waymarked trails: The Rowan Trail.

> **Enjoy some truly stunning views on this fascinating walk**

This walk from Chingford station takes in the Pole Hill obelisks, which mark the Greenwich Meridian, and stunning views over London and the Forest. It passes through groves of twisted hornbeam to the open expanse of Yates' Meadow, a mass of flowers in May and June and impressive throughout the year. Pole Hill has literary associations too: T. E. Lawrence, 'Lawrence of Arabia', owned land on Pole Hill and was associated with a temporary dwelling there known as The Cloisters.

Pole Hill and Yates' Meadow

Pole Hill

Route instructions

A Leave Chingford Rail Station and turn right towards the Forest. Turn left into Bury Road and then left onto the surfaced horse ride, keeping the golf course on your right. As the ground rises, the path bends to the right. Here bear left onto the smaller track leading straight ahead to the ridge of the hill.

1 Chingford Golf Course dates back to 1886 and is a public course laid out on Forest land. It is one of the oldest courses in the country. In the Second World War a small prisoner of war camp with its own chapel was located here. The buildings were later used as a school before demolition in the 1950s.

B Continue through the trees towards a grassy glade where you will see two obelisks, a bench, and the distant view of the world-famous London skyline. Continue down the hill with a view of the reservoirs ahead of you, until you reach the houses.

2 The larger obelisk was erected in 1824 by the Astronomer Royal, John Pond, to mark the direction of true north from the Greenwich Observatory as can be read on the plaque. The Meridian was recalculated in 1850. The smaller obelisk marks the modern line of zero longitude.
T. E. Lawrence, whose First World War exploits earned him fame as 'Lawrence of Arabia', owned some of the land here. Lawrence and his his friend, Vyvyan Richards, a teacher at nearby Bancroft's School, dreamed of setting up a printing press and built a small hut

Plan your walk

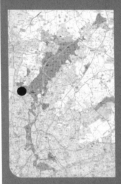

DISTANCE:
4 miles (6.2 km)

TIME:
1.75 hours

START/END:
Chingford Rail Station

PARKING:
Chingford Plain car park

TERRAIN:
Steep in places

NEAREST STATION:
Chingford Rail Station

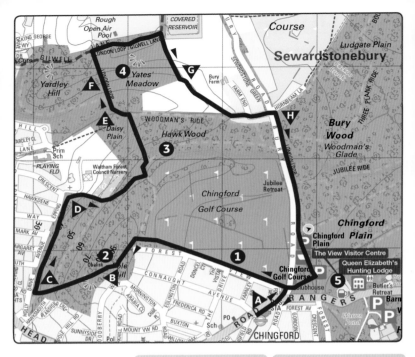

here. He left the hut and land to the local council who passed it on to Epping Forest in the early 1930s.

C Follow the track right skirting the perimeter of the Forest.

D Where the track comes to a right angle, follow it uphill through the trees, ignoring smaller paths leading downwards. You will reach a meeting of tracks, where a grassy horse ride leads steeply downhill.

3 This area is called Hawk Wood, the grassy ride is Daisy Plain. Note the many hornbeam pollards. Hornbeam has a silvery bark and a leaf similar to that of beech but more toothed. The name refers to the hardness of its wood, horn meaning hard and baum the old English for tree.

E Daisy Plain opens out as you descend. You will see two fields rising above you: Yardley Hill to the left, Yates' Meadow to the right. Look for wooden railings that mark a track leading

Pole Hill and Yates' Meadow

out of the Plain. Go through and take the right turn into Yates' Meadow.

▶ Keep parallel with the hedge to your left and continue along the top of the ridge. At the far corner turn right and head down the the hill.

4 Yates' Meadow is managed by seasonal mowing to encourage a mass of meadow flowers in the early summer. From the top ridge you can look over the Forest back to Pole Hill and its poplars, which appear in photographs of the hut where T. E. Lawrence stayed.

▶ Leave Yates' Meadow at the lower eastern corner through the wooden gate

marked with the London Loop arrow. The grassed path skirts left of a private field and then to the left of a farm gate onto Woodman Lane.

▶ Walk along Woodman Lane until you reach Bury Road. Cross the road and turn right onto the surfaced horse ride, which runs parallel to Bury Road, passing the car park and golf centre and back towards Chingford and the station.

5 As you come out onto the Plain, you will see Queen Elizabeth's Hunting Lodge to the left on the hill. Visit The Hunting Lodge and The View Visitor Centre, if you wish, or carry on to Rangers Road and back to the station.

Queen Elizabeth's Hunting Lodge

Yates' Meadow

66 A varied walk, taking in three of the Forest's premier locations: Queen Elizabeth's Hunting Lodge, Connaught Water and High Beach **99**

This is a circular walk from Queen Elizabeth's Hunting Lodge to Epping Forest Visitor Centre at High Beach. Queen Elizabeth's Hunting Lodge is a rare survival of a Tudor hunt standing and a 'must see' destination within Epping Forest.

Queen Elizabeth's Hunting Lodge to High Beach

Route instructions

A Turn right out of the gate at the rear of Queen Elizabeth's Hunting Lodge passing the rear of Butler's Retreat. Follow the grassy ride north-west down the slope with Butler's Pond on the right until you reach a surfaced ride.

1 Originally known as the Great Standing, Queen Elizabeth's Hunting Lodge is a unique and wonderful example of timber-framed architecture of the Tudor period. Built as a hunt standing (a sort of grandstand) in 1543 on the orders of King Henry VIII, the building was renovated in 1589 for Queen Elizabeth I.

B Cross the ride and take the path leading up a steep bank to Connaught Water.

2 This popular lake was named after the first Ranger of Epping Forest, the Duke of Connaught. It was once popular for skating in winter and boating in summer. Today Connaught Water is home to a variety of wildfowl including mandarin ducks, Canada geese, swans and great crested grebes. Skating is no longer permitted on the Forest's lakes and ponds.

C Turn right and follow the path, passing the car park, take the first path off to the right, heading north. The path briefly joins the easy access path by the boardwalk over Connaught Water. Bear right/straight on following the arrow on the waymarker post. Reaching Palmer's Bridge head north along the closed road to Fairmead car park.

3 Red Path is so named as when originally constructed, it was surfaced with crushed red bricks from local brickworks.

D Take the posted ride leading north out of the car park and up through Hill Wood. Bear left over the crest of the hill and continue down until it meets a surfaced ride.

4 On the flanks of the hill once stood the oldest hunting building in the Forest, New Lodge, first mentioned during Edward

DISTANCE:
6 miles (9 km)

TIME:
3 hours

START/END:
Queen Elizabeth's Hunting Lodge

PARKING:
Barn Hoppitt car park and Warren Pond car park

TERRAIN:
Mostly surfaced tracks and woodland trails

NEAREST STATION:
Chingford Rail Station

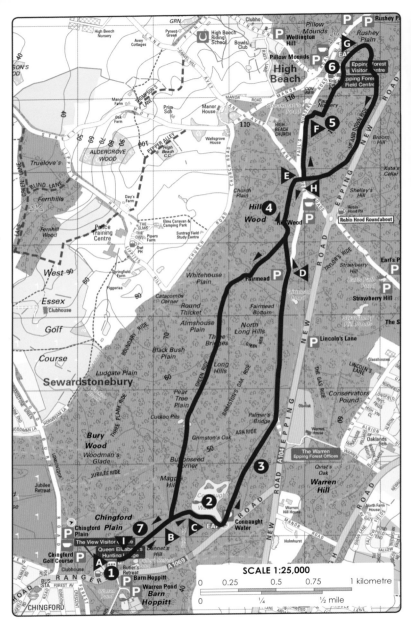

Queen Elizabeth's Hunting Lodge to High Beach

III's reign. Rebuilt in 1725 and then known as Fairmead Lodge, it later became the home of William Sotheby, who hosted a literary salon there attended by the Romantic Poets. When the Forest became public the Lodge was run as a tea room but was demolished soon after. Alongside was a famous ancient tree, the Fairmead Oak, from which the annual Easter Hunt took place until the 1880s. The tree was sadly destroyed by vandals in 1955. Nearby to the west of the hill and hidden within the depths of Hill Wood, is a Mesolithic flint workers' site.

E Turn right onto the surfaced ride and continue up the hill until it reaches the road. Cross the road and immediately turn left along a posted ride that follows Paul's Nursery Road.

F At the end of the ride (by a small brick building) follow the path to the right, running beside the Keeper's cottages. Veer left, through Paul's Nursery until you see a wooden fence line. Turn right and follow the fence to Epping Forest Visitor Centre at High Beach.

5 The brick built 'Potting Shed' is on the site of what was Paul's Nursery which extended behind the Keepers' cottages. Despite the 15 acres being added to the Forest in 1920, azaleas, Japanese maples and other exotic species can still be found.

6 Epping Forest Visitor Centre is built on the site of Britain's first speedway track. The bank of the old speedway may be seen in places encircling the site.

G On leaving the Visitor Centre turn right onto the easy access path. Keep turning right onto the surfaced Up and Down Ride, the reason behind the name of which will soon become apparent! Follow the ride until you reach the road.

H Cross the road diagonally right to the barrier gate and continue on the surfaced ride. At the bottom of the hill, the ride bends sharply to the right and then to the left. Continue along the surfaced ride, heading directly south for around one mile until you come out onto Chingford Plain.

7 Chingford Plain is an expanse of open grassland thought to be part of the deer park in Tudor times. It was enclosed and farmed in the mid 19th Century.

I Take the right-hand path, leading up the hill to Queen Elizabeth's Hunting Lodge and the start of the walk.

Epping Forest Visitor Centre at High Beach

> **"** This easy walk will take you around tranquil Connaught Water, with a chance to enjoy its wonderful birdlife **"**

The purpose-built easy access path encircling Connaught Water makes this walk fully accessible and is especially popular with young families or those with limited mobility. A boardwalk crosses part of the lake affording a stroll above the water. Connaught Water is perhaps one of the best lakes in Epping Forest to spot waterfowl including coots, swans, mandarin ducks and great crested grebes.

Runner enjoying Connaught Water

Connaught Water

Route instructions

A From the car park follow the lake round to the left, and admire the views over the lake.

1 Originally created in 1883 to drain a marshy part of the Forest, it was enlarged ten years later when the islands were created. Connaught Water was named after the first Ranger of the Forest, Queen Victoria's son, Arthur, Duke of Connaught. Like many of the Forest's ponds and lakes, Connaught Water was dug out by hand. Initially it was used as a paddling pond, but in 1888 a Miss Searle was granted the concession to provide rowing boats – an activity which continued until the mid 1970s. The lake is not very deep and in the much colder winters of the early 20th century frequently froze solid. This provided an opportunity for skaters to show off their skills and warm themselves with hot drinks supplied by Mr Butler from his marquee; his family also ran Butler's Retreat along Rangers Road. Boating and skating are no longer permitted.

Plan your walk

DISTANCE:
⅔ mile (1 km)

TIME:
½ hour

START/END:
Connaught Water car park

PARKING:
Connaught Water car park

TERRAIN:
Level surfaced track

NEAREST STATION:
Chingford Rail Station (½ hr walk)

Summer flowers at Connaught Water

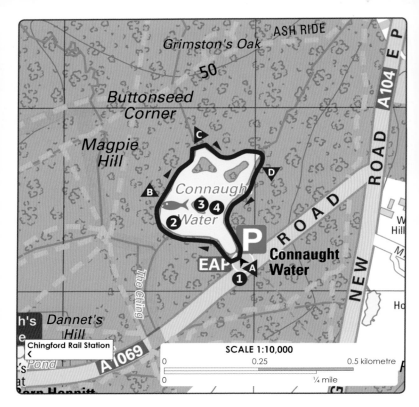

B Follow the path, passing the wooden angling platforms en route.

2 For many years the lake has proved to be popular with anglers and the health of the fish stocks is carefully monitored. The lake margin is fringed with willows, water mint and water forget-me-not. A number of accessible angling platforms are in place.

C When the junction with the boardwalk is reached, either turn right and cross the lake via the boardwalk or continue along the easy access path.

3 Connaught Water provides food and nesting sites for many different bird species including great crested grebes, mute swans, mallards, coots and moorhens. Brilliantly-coloured mandarin ducks

Connaught Water

often gather at the northern end of the lake during the winter months and in summer common terns may pay a fleeting visit to fish in the clean waters of the lake.

4 Several species of dragonfly hawk over Connaught Water and the emerging swarms of mayflies and midges provide ample food for bats on warm summer evenings.

▷ Keep following the easy access path to the car park and the start of the walk.

Black-tailed skimmer (female)

Shoveller

Tufted duck

Frog

" A charming introduction to Epping Forest "

This walk route, close to the Forest town of Loughton with its excellent public transport links and vibrant High Street, provides a pleasant taste of what Epping Forest has to offer with much of its ancient woodland bordering urban areas, towns and village.

Strawberry Hill Pond

Fly agaric, Strawberry Hill Pond

Route instructions

A Leaving Loughton Underground Station behind, head up Station Road to the High Street. Turn left along the High Street and cross over to Ollards Grove, taking the almost immediate right turn up Connaught Avenue to The Stubbles car park.

1 At the top of Station Road and the junction of the High Street stands a fine red brick building, Lopping Hall. Designed by Edmund Egan, it was built with part of the £7,000 Loughton received from the City of London Corporation as compensation for the loss of its lopping rights, when the Forest was acquired by the City of London Corporation under the Epping Forest Act of 1878.

2 The former enclosure known as The Stubbles, was ploughed until the late 1800s. Ridge and furrow lines can still be seen across the open grassland.

Plan your walk

DISTANCE:
2.5 miles (4 km)

TIME:
1.5 hours

START/END:
Loughton Underground Station

PARKING:
Strawberry Hill Pond car park or Earl's Path car park

TERRAIN:
Natural woodland/ surfaced horse rides

NEAREST STATION:
Loughton Underground Station

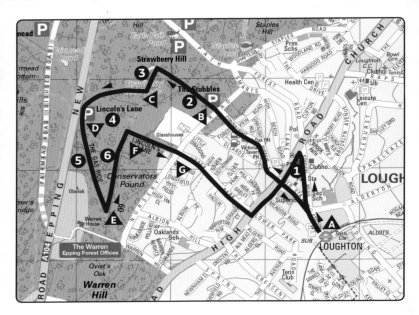

B From the car park head north-west across the open ground of The Stubbles until you meet a surfaced ride by Strawberry Hill Pond. Then turn left onto the surfaced ride and head south.

3 Strawberry Hill Pond is one of the prettiest ponds in the Forest. It provides an excellent habitat for many different species of birds, mammals and insects. Daubenton, noctule and pipistrelle bats may be seen hunting across its waters on a mild evening. The many ancient trees in the area offer excellent roost sites.

C Carry on along the surfaced ride which bears right, leading to the car park on the Epping New Road.

4 In winter, the mixed woodland along this stretch can seem alive with twittering blue tits and long-tailed tits that seem to flutter along just ahead of one's tracks.

D At the car park, turn left and follow The Gas Ride.

5 The Gas Ride gained its unglamorous name due to the gas pipe that runs underneath the length of the ride.

Strawberry Hill Pond

E Some 400 metres along The Gas Ride, look out for the unsurfaced horse ride that spurs off to the left. Turn left here.

6 Along this ride, much management work is carried out to promote the habitat for song birds such as nightingales. Although nightingales do sing during the day the best time to hear their ethereal song is in the quiet and still of the night.

F Head along the track until you see an open grassy area on the left and the unsurfaced ride of the eastern end of Lincoln's Lane on the right. Turn right here and carry on until you reach Nursery Road.

G Cross Nursery Road and head down Upper Park and back to the High Street. Turn left at the High Street until you reach Old Station Road and retrace your steps back to the station.

Strawberry Hill Pond

> **Explore the historic woodlands and ancient grasslands overlooked by Queen Elizabeth's Hunting Lodge**

This walk explores one of the Forest's most popular areas. With magnificent Queen Elizabeth's Hunting Lodge at the crest of Dannetts Hill adjacent to Epping Forest's flagship Visitor Centre, The View, it is easy to see why it has been so popular with visitors for hundreds of years – particularly since its heyday with the arrival of the railway in 1878.

Bury Wood and Chingford Plain

Picnic at Dannet's Hill

Plan your walk

DISTANCE:
2.7 miles (4.1 km)

TIME:
1.25 hours

START/END:
Chingford Plain car park

PARKING:
Chingford Plain car park

TERRAIN:
Mixture of surfaced tracks and woodland trails

NEAREST STATION:
Chingford Rail Station

Route instructions

A Leaving Chingford Plain car park, take the surfaced path that leads to Bury Wood.

1 Epping Forest has many old trees which are essential for wildlife such as bats, birds, insects, fungi and mosses. Many of these trees have been pollarded. This was a process where the tree was cut at head height when young. This promoted the growth of branches from the cut point. These branches were cut repeatedly on a 15 to 20 year cycle. In this way wood was harvested. Now the trees are managed for their wildlife value rather than wood production. Many of the pollards have not been cut for over 100 years and the branches are now as big as individual trees.

B Follow the surfaced ride alongside Bury Road until you reach the end of the ride. Turn right onto Boundary Ride. Pass over a small stream, Cuckoo Brook, which feeds into The Ching, which flows through Chingford.

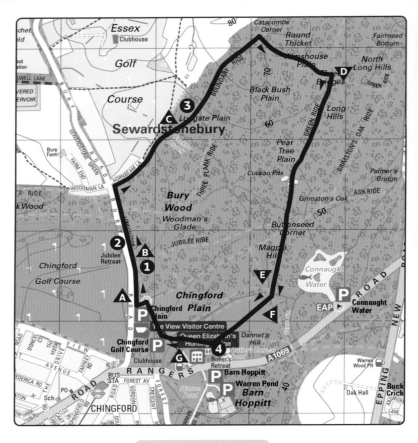

2 Halfway along Bury Road you will spot the buildings of the former Jubilee Retreat. This was one of the many wooden buildings in the Forest providing refreshment and recreation to the hordes of visitors who came on organised excursions before the Second World War. It was then surrounded by a fairground with a helter skelter.

C Follow the ride, passing Ludgate Plain, head up the hill and take the next surfaced path on the right, crossing Almshouse Plain.

3 The grassland area of Ludgate Plain supports a thriving colony of bird's-foot-trefoil and many of the mature trees in the area have been reduced to prolong their lives and

Bury Wood and Chingford Plain

to promote the growth of the ground flora. Many of the young trees have been made into new pollards.

D Follow the ride round to the right and head south along The Green Ride.

E Go straight over at the junction of rides and take the path approximately 15m ahead on the right.

F Follow this path to Chingford Plain and then follow the posted ride up the hill to Queen Elizabeth's Hunting Lodge and Butler's Retreat.

4 Butler's Retreat is a 19th-century barn converted into a tea house. In 1891 John Butler took over the lease and added canvas covered shelters outside the building, providing seating for over 600 people. At that time, and for many years after, Epping Forest flourished as a 'Cockney paradise', a popular day out for vast numbers of visitors from London's East End.

G From the Hunting Lodge head down the hill to Chingford Plain car park and where you started the walk.

Chingford Plain

This is perhaps the quintessential Epping Forest walk. In part it follows a delightful meandering brook with ancient Loughton Camp and the beautiful Lost Pond, just a short detour off route. An insight into the strategic thinking behind the construction of Loughton Camp is given when one appreciates the climb to the top of the hill to the Camp's almost secret location. One also understands how the Lost Pond gained the name 'Lost' as the pond seems camouflaged amongst the trees.

Beech coppard

Loughton Camp and Loughton Brook

The Lost Pond

Route instructions

A From Loughton Underground Station take Station Road to Loughton High Road. Cross to the police station and head up Forest Road. Turn right into Shaftesbury and take the steps on the left, up the side of the dam, to Staples Pond.

B Follow the woodland trail to the left from the top of the dam straight ahead and uphill then bear right on a wide path until you reach the surfaced Green Ride and turn right.

1 Originally called 'Victoria's Ride', The Green Ride was constructed in 1882. It is said that it was intended for Queen Victoria's visit to Epping Forest that year, but as she travelled from Chingford only to High Beach, she never used it.

C Continue on The Green Ride up a steep hill until you reach the small open green of Sandpit Plain on the right.

Pause to visit Loughton Camp by taking one of the small winding paths that spur off to the left, opposite Sandpit Plain. The start of the ramparts are just 2-3 minutes walk from the ride.

A detour to the Lost Pond may be taken by following one of the small paths heading north-east from Sandpit Plain. The pond is just a 4-5 minute walk from Sandpit Plain.

Plan your walk

DISTANCE:
2.5 miles (4 kms)

TIME:
1.5 hours

START/END:
Loughton Underground Station

PARKING:
Earl's Path car park

TERRAIN:
Undulating natural woodland

NEAREST STATION:
Loughton Underground Station

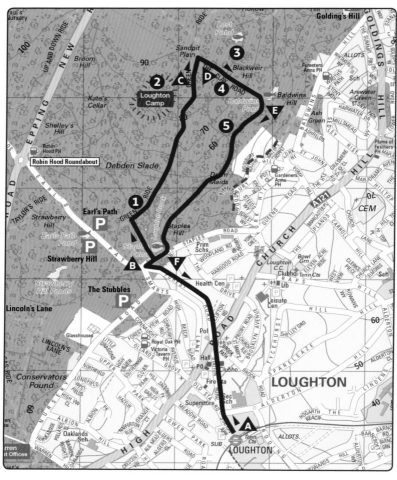

2 Loughton Camp is thought to be an Iron Age hill fort. It has been dated at around 300 BC or slightly earlier. Although we cannot be certain, it is generally believed that this, and nearby Ambresbury Banks, were used as refuges during times of conflict. This could well be one of the British strongholds that Caesar wrote about in his report of his invasion of Britain '*strongholds hidden in densely wooded spots fortified by a rampart and ditch, to which they retire in order to escape the attacks of invaders*'. Set above a steep valley and hidden among the trees with a

Loughton Camp and Loughton Brook

spring inside the Camp providing drinking water, this would certainly have been an ideal site from a military perspective.

3 The Lost Pond, also known as Blackweir Pond, is one of the most picturesque of all Forest ponds. Like all Forest ponds and lakes, the Lost Pond is man-made, the remains of a gravel pit created in 1895 and used for local road making for two decades. Take time to admire one of the Forest's oldest trees, a beech coppard that is estimated to be around 1,000 years old – see photo on page 58.

▶ From Sandpit Plain head downhill along The Clay Road to Baldwins Pond.

4 The land having been illegally 'enclosed' by the Lord of the Manor of Loughton, the Clay Road was constructed in the mid 1860s and was intended to form a road from Loughton to High Beach. Plots of land beside the road were to be offered for sale as housing. Luckily, it was around this time that the legal battle to save the

Forest began and this area was saved from enclosure and development.

▶ At Baldwins Hill dam, head down the steep slope and follow either side of meandering Loughton Brook back to Staples Pond.

5 The feeder springs to Loughton Brook start at High Beach and form into small streams which flow into the Loughton Brook valley cutting down into the London Clay. All the streams in the immediate area flow into Loughton Brook, through Loughton and into the River Roding. The Brook is a Regionally Important Geomorphological Site (RIGS) because of the meandering channels which have carved a classically sinuous 'wave' along this stretch. A dry 'ox-bow' (an isolated meander) can be seen along one stretch of the Brook.

▶ From Staples Pond retrace your steps to Loughton Underground Station.

Beech

66 High Beach has been enduringly popular with Forest visitors for centuries and is often thought of as the 'heart' of the Forest **99**

Starting at Epping Forest Visitor Centre at High Beach, this walk covers a circular route around High Beach, a beautiful and historic area, passing High Beach Church along the way.

View from the Pillow Mounds

Around High Beach

Route instructions

▶ On leaving Epping Forest Visitor Centre, turn right onto the Easy Access Path, just past the gate.

1 Epping Forest Visitor Centre is operated by volunteers from Epping Forest Heritage Trust, on behalf of the City of London Corporation.

B Keep to the left and you will pass Oak Plain Pond (on your left). When you reach the larger surfaced horse ride turn left and follow the ride to the road.

C Cross the road and head towards the green tea hut by the Pillow Mounds.

2 The Pillow Mounds are the remains of an artificial rabbit warren; rabbit fur and meat was once considered valuable.

Plan your walk

DISTANCE:
2.2 miles (3.8 km)

TIME:
1.5 hours

START/END:
Epping Forest Visitor Centre

PARKING:
Pillow Mounds car park

TERRAIN:
Mixture of surfaced tracks and woodland trails

NEAREST STATION:
Loughton Underground Station

High Beach

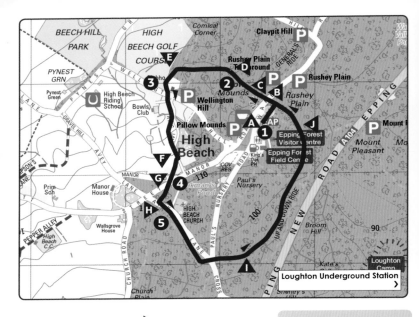

D Following the path behind the tea hut, head down the hill. Towards the bottom, take the left hand fork in the path leading to a bridge crossing the stream and head towards the car park.

E Walk along the boundary fence of the pub on your right, cross the road and enter Rats Lane. Follow Rats Lane and then continue along a woodland path backing onto gardens and heading up a steep hill.

3 Epping Forest was once a popular haunt for highwaymen. The notorious Dick Turpin frequented this area. He is said to have shot

a Forest Keeper in 1737 and nearby, hidden under one of the local houses, is the cave reputed to have been his hideout. His hideout is more likely to have been at Loughton Camp. The last recorded highway robbery in Epping Forest took place in 1837.

F Turn right onto Manor Road and then almost immediately take the left hand road opposite Arabin House and walk to the church.

4 High Beach Church (the Church of the Holy Innocents) was built in 1873, funded by Thomas Baring of nearby Wallsgrove

Around High Beach

House as a memorial to his two sons who had died in infancy. You can find the Baring family crypt in the north-west corner of the churchyard. The spire of the church rises to 38 metres (125 ft). Buried in the graveyard is the journalist and author of 'slum literature' Arthur Morrison, who lived at Arabin House.

G Continue past the church and at the T-junction, cross Avey Lane and enter the Forest. You will soon reach an unsurfaced horse ride.

5 Human occupation of this area has been shaping the landscape since the Stone Age. Microliths have been found in the Forest south of the church. These small sharp pieces of flint were used with resin to make tools.

H Turn left here and follow the ride, running parallel to the road until you meet a surfaced horse ride. Turn left to the barrier gate and cross the road.

I Follow the aptly named Up and Down Ride to where the surfaced ride forks.

J Take the left fork and carry straight on until you reach Epping Forest Visitor Centre at High Beach.

Great Spotted Woodpecker

Rabbit

" A varied walk starting just outside the village of Theydon Bois heading into deep ancient woodland, passing the Deer Sanctuary en route "

This walk heads off-track through what is perhaps some of the most beautiful woodland in Epping Forest. Many ancient beech, hornbeam and oak pollards are to be seen along the way. The route passes the Deer Sanctuary, where it may be possible to catch a glimpse of the Sanctuary's resident fallow deer.

Fallow doe

Deer Sanctuary

Near Hatgate Plain

Route instructions

A From Jack's Hill car park, follow the Ditches Ride for approximately 400m until you see a post with an arrow on the left.

1 Running alongside the eastern flank of the Ditches Ride is a Second World War tank defence ditch and bank. The bank was constructed by the local Home Guard in preparedness for a possible German invasion.

B Follow the winding horse ride until you reach a stream in a hollow. Look for the waymarked bridleway symbol, keeping the stream on your left.

2 The bridleway has some magnificent old ash trees growing on the bank adjoining Birch Wood.

C Follow the bridleway marker running alongside Debden Campsite.

Plan your walk

DISTANCE:
2.5 miles (4.5 km)

TIME:
1.5 hours

START/END:
Jack's Hill car park

PARKING:
Jack's Hill car park

TERRAIN:
Mixture of surfaced tracks and woodland trails

NEAREST STATION:
Theydon Bois Underground Station

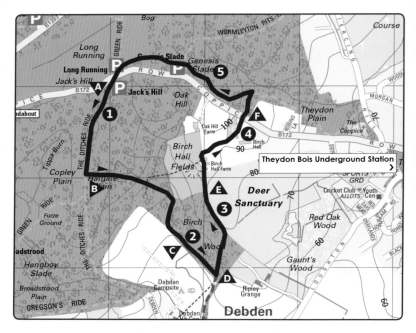

D At the T-junction by a wire fence, turn left and head up the hill to the Deer Sanctuary.

3 Surrounded by a high wire fence this area provides safe grazing for around 100 fallow deer. In the late 1950s the Conservators became increasingly concerned about the number of deer being killed on Forest roads. The Deer Sanctuary was established in 1959 to retain specimens of the dark coloured deer which have long been associated with Epping Forest.

E With the Deer Sanctuary fence on your right, follow the track, passing the wooden gate and enter a surfaced private road past Birch Hall to Coppice Row.

4 The palatial Birch Hall was built in the early 1990s on the site of an earlier house of the same name which was, for a long time, home to the Buxton family.

F Cross the road and follow the informal Forest path until it meets a surfaced ride. Turn left onto the ride and proceed to the

Deer Sanctuary

second of two car parks, and cross the road back to Jack's Hill car park.

5 The woodland at Genesis Slade consists predominantly of towering unpollarded beech, with some oak and a smaller amount of hornbeam and holly. Birch invasion has occurred in patches. North of Genesis Slade is an area of overgrown beech coppice which gives its name to Coppice Row.

View from Birch Hill

66 Copped Hall Park, with its landmark-ruined mansion, often glimpsed when travelling on the M25, is hauntingly inviting to visit **99**

This walk from Long Running car park to Copped Hall explores the contrast between Epping Forest's ancient woodlands and the estate and agricultural landscape of the Copped Hall estate, now part of the Buffer Lands owned and managed by the City of London Corporation. The walk provides an opportunity to see wild fallow deer, particularly at dusk or dawn on open land around Copped Hall.

Copped Hall

Boxing hares

Route instructions

A Head north along the ride from Long Running car park and take the first left turn towards Epping New Road.

1 The woodland surrounding the open heathland of Long Running contains some magnificent ancient trees, many of which are pollards or coppards. Coppards are formerly coppiced trees that have been allowed to grow tall enough to be pollarded.

B Cross the busy road with care and turn left until you reach disused Lodge Road. Turn right, passing Lodge Road car park, and continue until you see the entrance gates to Copped Hall across Crown Hill Road.

2 Lodge Road passes two valley bogs of great conservation importance. Both exist because a road was constructed across two springs, causing ponding. Analysis of the mud layers of the bogs suggests that a track was created here in the late Neolithic period or early Bronze Age.

C Pass through the left hand gate and go straight ahead along the drive through the Warren Plantation, crossing the

Plan your walk

DISTANCE:
4 miles (6.2 km)

TIME:
2.25 hours

START/END:
Long Running car park or Lodge Road car park

PARKING:
Long Running car park or Lodge Road car park

TERRAIN:
Mostly surfaced tracks

NEAREST STATION:
Unfortunately, this walk is not well served by public transport

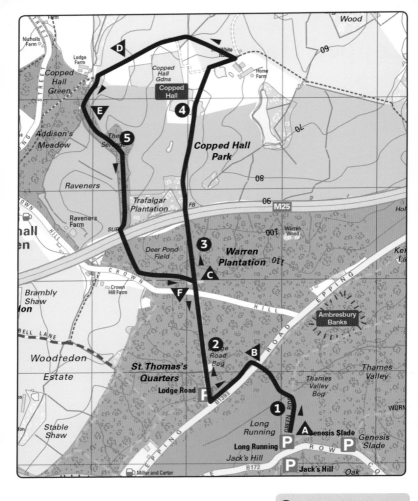

bridge over the M25 and passing the front of Copped Hall mansion, until you meet a small estate road. Turn right and after 100m turn left at The White House and cross the stile into the field.

3 The Warren Plantation, either side of the drive, includes at least 60 different species of trees. Fallow deer are common in this area and may often be glimpsed through the trees.

Copped Hall

4 The magnificent Copped Hall mansion dates from the 1750s. Burned out in 1917, it is being restored to its former glory by the Copped Hall Trust. On the site was a medieval palace owned by Waltham Abbey, which was replaced by a large Elizabethan house built by Sir Thomas Heneage. The present mansion is surrounded by agricultural land where lapwings may be seen feeding on the crops and hares dash across the fields.

D The public footpath takes a route diagonally across the farm field, with a great view of Copped Hall on the left, and joins a private road leading to the gates by Lodge Farm Stables. Turn left into The Selvage.

E Follow the path through The Selvage and go through the tunnel under the M25. Then head left across the field and up the hill to the Copped Hall gates once again.

5 The route takes you through 'The Selvage'. This is a landscape feature of the Copped Hall estate dating back to the early nineteenth century and planted with hazel coppice and conifers. The Deer Tunnel was constructed for the deer to pass safely under the M25.

F Retrace your steps back to Long Running car park and the end of the walk.

Yellowhammer

Copped Hall

> 66 Discover beautiful Epping Forest and some of its surrounding Buffer Lands by following the waymarked Oak Trail 99

This walk explores the contrast between Epping Forest's ancient woodlands and the agricultural landscape of Epping Forest's Buffer Land at Great Gregories.

Theydon to Epping ramble

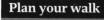

Route instructions

A Leaving the station, follow the waymark arrows leading from Station Approach, turning right into Forest Drive. At the the end of Forest Drive, continue following the waymark arrows.

1 Great Gregories is now part of the Buffer Lands, land purchased by the City of London Corporation to protect the Forest boundaries. Great Gregories, formerly part of a farm, was purchased in 1989. Mostly farmland, it now provides winter housing for the cattle who graze the Forest in the spring and summer each year.

B Following the footpath, head across the M25 bridge and up through Sheppard's Meadow to Bell Common.

2 Sheppard's Meadow was added to the Forest in 1991, as 'exchange lands for land lost to the M25'. With its long history of grazing, it is a good place to look for spring and summer flowers and butterflies.

3 Bell Common, formerly known as Beacon Common, was an important grazing stop for drovers leading their cattle into London. The Bell Hotel opposite used to be called the Drovers Inn for that reason.

Plan your walk

DISTANCE:
7 miles (11 km)

TIME:
3 hours

START/END:
Theydon Bois
Underground Station

PARKING:
Forest Side, Jack's Hill, Long Running or Epping Cricket Ground car parks

TERRAIN:
Hilly ground, mostly on good tracks

NEAREST STATION:
Theydon Bois
Underground Station

Muntjac

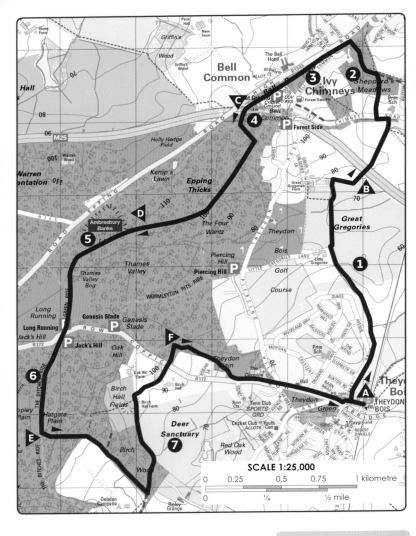

C Skirting around the cricket ground head south towards Epping Thicks.

4 During the construction of the M25 in the 1980s, Epping Forest was under threat of the motorway being cut across the Forest. Following much

Theydon to Epping ramble

campaigning, it was agreed to tunnel the motorway under the Forest here at Epping. The cricket pitch was replaced on top of the tunnel making it one of the most expensive cricket grounds in the country.

▶ Keeping to the surfaced ride, head south, detouring to visit Ambresbury Banks, en route.

5 Owing to its great earth banks, you'll spot Ambresbury Banks from the main ride on your right. Rumoured to have been the camp of Queen Boudica, there is no evidence she lived here or that there was any long term occupation. It seems it was a place of refuge in times of trouble. Great beeches now dominate the area.

6 The raised earthworks to your right, running alongside the ride, are the remains of an anti-tank ditch that was dug by the local Home Guard during the Second World War, when measures were undertaken to prepare for the potential threat of German invasion.

▶ Re-joining the waymarked trail, cross Coppice Row and follow the ride until you see the arrow pointing east, where you leave the surfaced ride and head into the trees towards the Deer Sanctuary.

7 The Deer Sanctuary is home to some 100 fallow deer and was established to protect this particular strain of dark coloured fallow.

▶ Crossing Coppice Row once again, turn right to reach the start of the walk.

English Longhorn cow

> **❝** A beautiful walk that winds and twists through some of the loveliest parts of Epping Forest **❞**

This walk covers a multitude of different terrain and leads one through some of the less well-known parts of Epping Forest. There is always the enticing promise of a glimpse of the Forest's fallow deer whilst buzzards soar and mew overhead. Do take time to pause en route at some of the history woven into the Forest landscape.

Rifle Butts – Wake Valley Pond

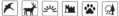

Route instructions

A From Honey Lane car park head up the Rifle Butts Ride and turn right at the top of Flagstaff Hill.

1 The steep hill forming the Rifle Butts was used for target training from the Napoleonic War through to the Second World War. Discarded shells can still be found in the area. Some 20 years ago, Forest woodmen working at the site were dismayed to find that two of their chainsaws became mysteriously jammed when cutting one of the trees. Upon further investigation, the trunk of the tree was found to be crammed full of metal shot.

B Follow the ride across Claypit Hill Road onto the General's Ride.

2 At the top of the Rifle Butts is Flagstaff Hill which got its name from the red flag that used to be flown when target practice was being carried out. It is said that the Forest Superintendent of the time was obliged to give permission for the flagstaff to be erected due to complaints received from walkers suffering near misses.

3 Beside The General's Ride some magnificent ancient pollards can be

Plan your walk

DISTANCE:
4 miles (6.2 km)

TIME:
2 hours

START/END:
Honey Lane car park or Wake Valley Pond car park

PARKING:
Honey Lane car park or Wake Valley Pond car park

TERRAIN:
Mixture of surfaced tracks and woodland trails

NEAREST STATION:
Unfortunately, this walk is not well served by public transport

Remains of a rifle butt

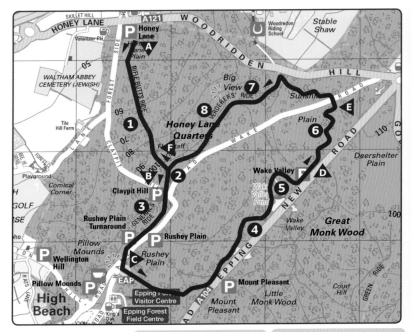

seen, one of which has the nickname of 'Big Tom', although no one knows how it earned this name.

C At the end of the General's Ride cross Manor Road and follow the ride to just before the Epping New Road. Go through the access point in the fencing and take the unmarked woodland trail that winds its way past Little Wake Pond and The Bomb Crater Pond to Wake Valley Pond.

4 The Bomb Crater Pond was caused by the explosion of a parachute land-mine in 1940.

5 Beautiful Wake Valley Pond is one of the deepest of the Forest's ponds and was used as a swimming pool and even had diving boards until, following several drownings, swimming was banned in all Forest ponds. Today it is a popular angling lake.

D Go through the car park and follow the woodland trail that snakes its way across Sunshine Plain.

6 Sunshine Plain is an area of wet heathland and an excellent spot to look out for the Forest's dark fallow deer that invariably frequent this spot.

Rifle Butts – Wake Valley Pond

▶ Cross Wake Road and continue across the open glade until you meet the surfaced Verderers' Ride. Turn left and detour to admire Big View on the right.

7 Verderers' Ride is named after the ancient role of Forest Verderer. The office was first introduced almost 1000 years ago. Verderers were judges in forest courts. The name was retained when the Epping Forest Act was passed in 1878 but today's four elected Verderers have no judicial role. They represent the interests of the Forest's Commoners (and the local public) on the Committee that oversees the Forest.

8 Big View provides an extensive panorama across the Lea Valley to the hills of Hertfordshire. The Abbey Church can be seen nestled within historic Waltham Abbey.

▶ At Flagstaff Hill turn right and head back down the Rifle Butts to the start of the walk.

Wake Valley Pond

This fascinating old park offers some great views and good open walking

This circular walk explores some of the undulating pastoral parkland of Warlies Park. The Woodredon and Warlies Park Estate passed into the ownership of the City of London Corporation in 1986 and forms part of the Buffer Lands. The Park is criss-crossed with public footpaths, permissive footpaths and a public bridleway.

Warlies Park

Summer grass at Warlies Park

Route instructions

A Take the footpath to the right of the Upshire Village Hall enclosure and follow the path ahead.

1 In 1853, Warlies Park was purchased by the Buxton family who added various features, including Cobbin Pond. In 1921 the house and gardens were sold to Dr Barnardo's Homes whilst the remainder of the Estate was retained by the Buxton family until 1974, when it and the adjoining Woodredon Estate were sold to the Greater London Council and then acquired by the City of London Corporation.

B Take a short detour to admire The Temple at the crest of the hill where there is a nice view over the countryside. Carry on round the edge of the gardens to the house by the small pond.

Plan your walk

DISTANCE:
2 miles (3.2 km)

TIME:
1 hour

START/END:
Horseshoe Hill, Upshire

PARKING:
Fernhall Lane car park, parking is limited so please note that the start of the walk is near the Village Hall .

TERRAIN:
Mostly grassy trails

NEAREST STATION:
Unfortunately, this walk is not well served by public transport

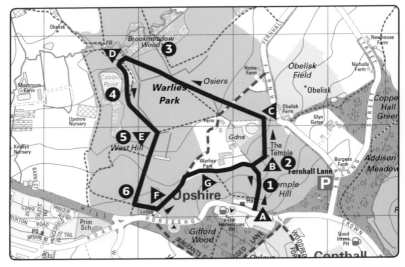

2 The Park contains a number of interesting historic features, including a rotunda known as The Temple, which is a Scheduled Ancient Monument.

C Cross the Bridleway and then take the footpath north-west toward the edge of Brookmeadow Wood.

3 The blocks of woodland surrounding the Park provide wildlife links with the adjacent farmland and northern parts of Epping Forest.

D Turn left and follow the path to the corner of the field and the edge of Cobbin Pond.

4 Cobbin Pond provides a valuable wildlife habitat for many species of waterfowl.

E Follow the path to the trees at the crest of the hill, turning left at point 6 on the map.

5 During the summer months, wild flowers including agrimony, cuckoo flower, ox-eye daisy, ragged robin and some cowslips may be seen in much of the Park.

F Head towards the gate where the footpath crosses the old cricket pitch and meets the private road. Turn left and head toward the old entrance to Warlies House. Take the footpath through the small gate on the right.

Warlies Park

6 Little owls, jackdaws and starlings nest in many of the Park's old trees and skylarks sing overhead in summer.

G Follow the path along the boundary of Warlies House to the first right-hand turn. Head back to the Village Hall and the start of the walk.

A summer evening in Warlies Park

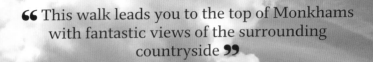

> **"** This walk leads you to the top of Monkhams with fantastic views of the surrounding countryside **"**

Monkhams is one of the lesser known and quieter parts of Epping Forest. At the crest of Monkhams Hill, which forms part of Epping Forest's nearly 2000 acres of Buffer Land, lies the remains of a gun emplacement which was used during both the First World War and the Second World War.

Gun emplacement, Monkhams

Monkhams

Route instructions

A From Aimes Green take the Public Bridleway, Clapgate Lane, until you reach the entrance to the grassy expanse of Monkhams on the right.

1 Monkhams forms part of the City of London's Buffer Land, acquired by the City of London to protect Epping Forest from encroaching development and to maintain the links between the Forest and the wider countryside. Lying to the south of Monkhams and forming part of Epping Forest, Clapgate Lane is one of a number of old drove roads in the area.

B Head across the open field to the crest of the hill.

2 The gun emplacement at the summit of Monkhams offers a commanding view over London and much of Hertfordshire. Embedded in the centre of the brick

Plan your walk

DISTANCE:
1.75 miles (2.8 km)

TIME:
1 hour

START/END:
Aimes Green

PARKING:
Aimes Green

TERRAIN:
Undulating unsurfaced ground

NEAREST STATION:
Unfortunately, this walk is not well served by public transport

Monkhams

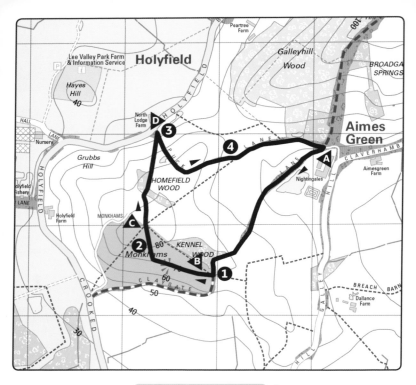

structure, by the remains of a brick building, is a six-foot diameter steel gun mounting plate. This site leaves one in no doubt of the strategically important position that this gun emplacement held in the protection of London and the nearby Royal Gunpowder Factory at Waltham Abbey. Close to the remains of the gun emplacement is an Ordnance Survey triangulation survey point at 271 feet above sea level.

C Head north towards the junction of the four public footpaths and take the left footpath north to Puck Lane.

3 Puck Lane is another of the Forest's green lanes with a public bridleway running along it. At the western end of Puck Lane lies a puddingstone. These natural conglomerate boulders have been found placed in significant old route-ways across the southeast. They are thought to have been Neolithic track markers.

Monkhams

▶ Turn right and follow Puck Lane back to Aimes Green.

④ The mixed ancient hedgerows bordering old green lanes, such as this, provide great habitats for many species of bird such as dunnock, wren and song thrush.

Peacock butterfly

> **❝ This little known gem, lying to the north of Epping, is a delight to visit at any time of year ❞**

This triangular portion of Epping Forest covers 191 hectares. The woodlands are a mix of ash, hornbeam, oak and field maple with some hazel, hawthorn and holly. The heavy clay soils support a wealth of wild flowers and ferns including primroses, wood sorrel, wood sanicle, yellow pimpernel, violets and ragged robin. It is particularly rich in wildlife and a delight to explore.

Fallow buck

Lower Forest

Nuthatch

Route instructions

A From the The Woodyard car park, cross the road into the Lower Forest. Turn right and follow the unsurfaced ride with the road to your right. Ignore the ride that spurs off to the left and follow the ride until it meets the northern end of Wintry Wood Ride.

B Turn left onto Wintry Wood Ride for about 20 metres and take a small secretive winding track, not much more than a deer trail, through the trees, crossing a small stream en route until you reach the open grassland at the northern end of The Lower Forest.

1 One of the largest colonies of rooks in Essex is located in the north east corner of the Lower Forest. Their noisy cawing in the new year heralds the start of spring.

2 Wintry Wood appears in records from the 13th century and was mentioned in the perambulation of the Forest in 1301. Old maps indicate that there was a larger portion of woodland, to the west of Wintry Wood.

Plan your walk

DISTANCE:
2.5 miles (4 km)

TIME:
2 hours

START/END:
The Woodyard car park

PARKING:
The Woodyard car park

TERRAIN:
Natural woodland

NEAREST STATION:
Epping Underground Station

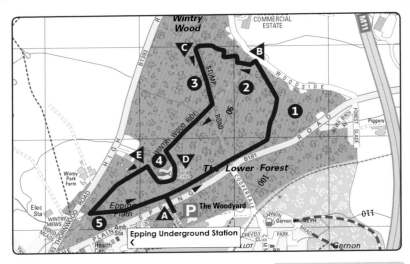

C Take the main track, the Stump Road, and head south to the crossroads and turn right along the Wintry Wood Ride.

3 The Stump Road was once part of the old road between London and Newmarket. To the north it connects with the main road to Harlow, and at the eastern end with the road to Coopersale. By 1833 the turnpike roads were established and ran either side of the Wood and the Stump Road dwindled in importance.

D After around 350 metres, detour off the ride and stroll around the lake.

4 Through a community project to relieve unemployment, local men dug out the lake in the winter of 1893/4. It was created as a place where people could swim in summer and skate in winter and was provided with a diving board, life buoys and a changing shed nearby. Today, no swimming or skating is allowed on any of the Forest's ponds for safety reasons.

E From The Lake, take the posted ride toward The Plain and make a sharp left, back to the start of the walk.

5 The maturing maiden oaks growing on the former open plain began to grow and spread across The Plain during the 1930s.

Lower Forest

Bee on primrose

What to look out for on your walk

Spring

- Bluebells – the best place to enjoy bluebells is Wanstead Park.

- Bird song – arrive in the Forest just before dawn to hear the dawn chorus.

- Hares – visit the Forest's Buffer Lands at Copped Hall to see the 'madness' of hares in March.

Summer

- Dragonflies and damselflies – pause at the Forest's lakes and ponds to watch the dragonflies and damselflies darting and skimming around.

- Cattle – cows are turned out across the Forest to graze over the summer months.

- Wildflowers – enjoy the splendour of the wildflowers, visit Fernhills and Trueloves.

Autumn

- Fungi – choose a morning shortly after damp weather to see fungi at their best.

- Autumn colour – Great Monk Wood, Hill Wood and Birch Wood are especially good for autumn colour.

- The rut – listen out for the bellowing and clashing antlers of the fallow bucks.

Winter

- Tracks – winter snow and mud best show off what animals are out and about.

- Robin – listen out for the cheerful song of the robin, one of the few birds to sing all year round.

- Evergreens – the evergreens, such as holly, ivy and butcher's broom, stand out amongst the bare-leaved deciduous trees.

Ways in which you can help support Epping Forest

Epping Forest is a Registered Charity and we are grateful for all the support received from our visitors throughout the year. There are several ways you can help us look after Epping Forest:

Volunteering
If you have some time to spare, how about joining our volunteer team? There is a volunteering role for everyone. For more information please visit www.cityoflondon.gov.uk/eppingforest

Join us on social media
If you love Epping Forest and would like to stay up to date with all the news and views straight from your favourite ancient woodland, why not follow / like us on social media?

🐦 @CoLEppingForest
📘 Epping Forest City of London
📷 coleppingforest

When you get out and about in the Forest, hopefully enjoying the walks from this book, we'd love to see your photographs on social media, so please use #EppingForest or make contact via the above pages.

Buy an Epping Forest memory in one of our shops
Purchase your cards, a gift and Forest produce from our retail areas at The View, The Temple and Epping Forest Visitor Centre at High Beach. Here you can find a combination of woodland inspired merchandise, products created by local craftspeople and Epping Forest produce including venison and beef (available at The View only).

Enjoy an Epping Forest event
A variety of events and activities are held throughout the seasons, from walks and talks to Open Air Theatre. Support our events and have fun too!

Sign-up to receive a free, seasonal Epping Forest magazine
Visit www.cityoflondon.gov.uk/eppingforest to enter your e-mail address to be the first to hear the latest news from the woods, by subscribing to the electronic version of the seasonal magazine 'Forest Focus'. The printed version of this magazine can be picked-up at The View, The Temple and Epping Forest Visitor Centre at High Beach, as well as at many locations throughout the local area. If you would like to promote your business in this publication, please contact epping.forest@cityoflondon.gov.uk

Visit us online
Stay up to date by visiting www.cityoflondon.gov.uk/eppingforest

Donate to your favourite Forest
Help us by popping something into one of the donation boxes located at the Visitor Centres, or leave a gift in your will.

Host your private event at Queen Elizabeth's Hunting Lodge
This spectacular Tudor hunt standing can be hired for exclusive use and we are also licensed to host weddings. To find out more visit www.cityoflondon.gov.uk/eppingforest

All profits made through retail, events, private hire, donations and advertising are directed straight back into caring for Epping Forest, for the benefit and enjoyment of future generations of people and wildlife.